1 MONTH OF
FREE
READING

at
www.ForgottenBooks.com

By purchasing this book you are eligible for one month membership to ForgottenBooks.com, giving you unlimited access to our entire collection of over 1,000,000 titles via our web site and mobile apps.

To claim your free month visit:
www.forgottenbooks.com/free227885

ISBN 978-0-484-36962-6
PIBN 10227885

This book is a reproduction of an important historical work. Forgotten Books uses
state-of-the-art technology to digitally reconstruct the work, preserving the original format
whilst repairing imperfections present in the aged copy. In rare cases, an imperfection in
the original, such as a blemish or missing page, may be replicated in our edition. We do,
however, repair the vast majority of imperfections successfully; any imperfections that
remain are intentionally left to preserve the state of such historical works.

Seeds of April's Sowing

BY

ADAH
LOUISE
SUTTON

MCMII

The SAALFIELD PUBLISHING CO.

CHICAGO   AKRON, OHIO   NEW YORK

COPYRIGHT, 1902,

BY

THE SAALFIELD PUBLISHING COMPANY

MADE BY
THE WERNER COMPANY
AKRON, OHIO

TO THE BELOVÈD

"You'll love me yet,
        and I can tarry

Your love's protracted growing;

    June reared that bunch
        of flowers you carry,

From seeds of April's sowing."

BROWNING

CONTENTS

CONTENTS

6

BALLADE OF YELLOW AND GREEN

When groves are green and hedges sprout,
    And yellow buttercups laugh in the lane,
When the dandelion shakes its soft plumes out,
    And fields are aglint with the gold of grain;
    When cowslips drift in an amber rain,
And yellow's the silk of the tasseled corn,
    O, who has the hardihood then to complain
That green's forsaken and yellow's forsworn?

When Spring awakes in a joyful rout,
    Daffodil, primrose, a gladsome train,
When the jonquil scatters its gems about
    And marigolds weave a glowing chain;
    When pansies shine on the lawns again
And tulips nod in the fragrant morn,
    O, who will subscribe to the old-time strain
That green's forsaken and yellow's forsworn?

When fringed chrysanthemums flaunt and flout,
    And musk runs wild in a golden vein,
When yellow laburnum nods without,
    And golden-rod glorifies field and plain;
    When marguerites lie like a topaz stain,
And tea-rose lifteth her slender thorn,
    O, where can a fancy like this obtain,
That green's forsaken and yellow's forsworn?

Prince of all colors that wax and wane,
    Emerald and gold are royal-born;
Let us rescind the old refrain,
    That green's forsaken and yellow's forsworn.

A VALENTINE

I SEND you roses for a valentine;
    They lift their dear, flushed faces for a kiss;
Give them, belovèd, the caress that should be mine,
    And, lest they die of such ecstatic bliss,

Gather them close, and the insensate things
    Shall thrill to life, beneath your awakening touch;
But oh, beware, lest roses, too, have hearts,
    And, waked to loving, worship overmuch.

The thought of you fills every waking hour,
    And peoples all the vista of my dreams,
And every prayer that does not tend toward thee,
    A wingless seraph, void and imperfect, seems.

So I send roses for a valentine;
    Smiling they go to play their lesser part;
For hidden within their glowing, fragrant bloom,
    I send a dearer gift,—a woman's heart.

ADIEU

IF I had not met thee,
Life had been less hard to bear;
How shall I forget thee?

When the dawn doth wake me,
From the night's long dreams of thee,
Thoughts of thee o'ertake me.

In the midnight splendor
Of the stars I see thine eyes,
Deep, and dark, and tender.

And the noontide glory
Whispers to my dreaming heart,
Just the same sweet story.

If I could forget thee,
Life would be less hard to bear;
Would I ne'er had met thee!

WHEN THE LIGHT GOES OUT

AN EASTER REVERIE

STILL graves on which the Easter lilies lie,
Pathetic mounds, 'neath an unbending sky,
 Whisper your dreams of rest to one who waits;
A slave who still works out his slavery.

Narrow the portal and the arch is low,
Whither it leadeth me, how shall I know?
 My feet are tired upon the hills of life;
To seek the untrodden path I fain would go.

The rugged way hath not been all unblessed,
Still have I never found things at their best;
 The Heart's Desire that I shall never see,
Hath stolen all the sweetness from the rest.

What is this change more than another one?
An hour to rest at setting of the sun
 Is kindly Death; a kiss on tired eyes,
And lying down to sleep when work is done.

None hath returned to tell of that far place
Toward which each man sets his unwilling face;
    What ardently he longs for, he believes,
And so believing still takes heart of grace.

This is that Faith whose crimson flag unfurled
Points still, above the shafts of vengeance hurled,
    An unruffled Deity who sits serene
And laughs across a topsy-turvy world.

Timid and faltering, still I shall not shrink;
'Tis easier than we dream or hope, I think;
    All that I need the most and cannot have,
Perhaps awaits me still beyond the Brink.

OUTWARD BOUND

I KNOW not where my haven lies,
　　Where that dear port of Peace may be;
I only trust 'neath happier skies,
　　A safer harbor waits for me,—
　　A sunlit heaven, a halcyon sea.

Somewhere there lies a zone of calm
　　Far from the reach of jar and fret,
'Neath airs that only breathe of balm,
　　Beyond the shadow of regret,—
　　That Golden Isle where we forget.

With his dear hand upon the helm,
　　The pilot I have waited for,
Through floods that leap to overwhelm,
　　Shall guide me to that peaceful shore,
　　Storm-tossed and tempest-driven no more.

So steadfastly I wait the hour
　　Till stars are high and tide runs free;
Patient although the tempest lower,
　　I dread no more the changing sea;
　　Somewhere my pilot waits for me.

SPRING-SONG

OVER our heads the branches meet,
    They sway together with soft caresses;
Golden mosses are under our feet,
    Fairy blooms that the sunshine blesses.
What can we ask from Earth or Heaven above?
Springtime is here, and thou and I, and *love*.

Spring again upon hill and stream,
    Mad with the joy of the world's recapture;
Ours, belovèd, this ecstatic dream,
    Half a regret and all a rapture.
What can we ask of God Himself above,
Since Spring is here, and thou and I, and *love?*

A TOAST

WHEN tired and discouraged I fly to my den,
And fasten the door against all sorts of men,
I find there in waiting a friend tried and true,
Whose presence brings courage when all things
look blue.

CHORUS

Here's to the friend that's unbiased by gold,
Here's to the mistress that never grows cold;
The jolly brown maiden who comes from afar!
Here's my Havana cigar!

Her touch is enchanting, her contact is bliss,
She presses my lips with a lingering kiss;
With tender caresses her smile I invoke,
And find all my troubles are ending in smoke.

So wrapt in a dream of Elysian delight,
I coquet with my charmer far into the night;
But she flees from my arms and I find for my
    pains,
That a heap of gray ashes is all that remains.

What damsel in petticoats e'er could compete,
With my glowing brown beauty so temptingly
    sweet?
And the best of it is, when she fades into air,
There's a boxful just like her awaiting me there.

AS ALL THE VILLAGE GOSSIPS SAY

IT HAPPENED on a summer day
    About a mile from town,
While soft gray eyes were looking up
    And brown eyes looking down;
That summer day, that golden day,
As all the village gossips say.

The path was but a narrow one
    O'erhead the branches met;
On either side sprang daisies pied,
    Wild rose and violet.
And so they loitered on the way,
As all the village gossips say.

A kiss is such a little thing
    When no one's by to see,
Except, perhaps, a wayside rose
    Or pink anemone.
It answered for this small delay,
As all the village gossips say.

But sweeter far another kiss
    Within the kirk at town,
While wedded eyes looked softly up
    As wedded eyes looked down.
And blessings on their bridal day! —
As all the village gossips say.

FRAUENLIEBE

LOVE unlocked the Gates of Heaven.
    "Enter thou alone."
"Hath my belovèd, then, no place
    Before the Great White Throne?"

Love unbarred the doors of Hell.
    "Enter, then, with him."
"Heaven without him had been void,
    Blessingless and dim."

THE EMPTY CRADLE

SHE came when daisies opened wide,
   And bluebells were in blossom,
And dimple-limbed and starry-eyed
   She nestled in her bosom.

She scarcely seemed a mortal thing,
   From her first opening hour;
More like an offering of the Spring,
   Some fair, frail, forest flower.

For all unuttered mysteries,
   To her sweet soul seemed given;
The light within her serious eyes
   Was less of Earth than Heaven.

She stayed with them through Autumn's hours,
   Through Winter's shine and shading,
But 'mid the Springtime's early flowers
   They knew that she was fading.

And e'er she learned to lisp one name,
 The sacred name of " Mother,"
The angel summons softly came
 To this world from the Other.

But still through all life's devious ways,
 Its shadows and repining,
The halo of those baby days
 Forever more is shining.

And from the veil that intervenes
 Twixt this world and that Other,
A little baby-angel leans,
 And softly whispers—" Mother ! "

A BACHELOR'S REASON

SHE'S rather faded now, and thin,
    Her shining locks are not so glossy;
She's lost the dimple in her chin,
    Her air's subdued, instead of saucy.
She's paler, too. The wild rose bloom,
    That used to make her such a beauty,
Has faded to make standing room
    For lines marked out by care and duty.

Her hand is not so plump and white,
    As on the day when first I pressed it;
But baby hands have clasped it tight,
    And baby lips in love caressed it.
A firm, warm hand, to shield and guide
    The little lives that must come after;
A tender heart to hold and hide
    The baby love and baby laughter.

I often see her pass this way,
    Her bright-eyed children clinging round her.
Oh, for the wasted yesterday,
    E'er yet another heart had found her!
It might have been! within my breast
    The secret grieving long hath tarried:
I wonder if she sometimes guessed
    The reason why I never married?

RENUNCIATION

My Heart's Desire hath flown away;
    I shall not find him any more,
In dull December or merry May,
    In leafy wood, by lonely shore,
At any time of night or day.

I cannot tell which way he went;
    He passed me like a flash of light,
With shadows all the sun was blent,
    And all the day pined into night,
And into grieving all content.

If he is happier otherwhere
    I would not wish him back again;
He filled my life with dear despair,
    Such tender tears, such passionate pain,
I would not call him back, my Fair.

If you should meet my Heart's Desire,
    I pray you let him go his way;
Though desolate lies my altar-fire,
    Though all my clouded skies are gray,
Although I touch a voiceless lyre.

BEFORE THE STORM

A LIVID sea, a lowering sky,
   A strip of leaden beach;
The wreck of a boat, flung high and dry,
And a sad-colored bird with a desolate cry,
   Flitting away out of reach.

A line of white on the sandy bar
   Where the fitful surf runs high;
A pallid mist rising near and far,
And the dream of a night without a star
   To enshroud it all, by and bye.

A WINTER SUNSET

THE sea glows like an amethyst
Against the horizon's scarlet rim,
And all the purple cliffs are dim,
Wrapped in a veil of pearly mist.

A white gull dips with sullen scream;
The rosy light is on his wings,
And on the gray mist's curling rings,
And land and sea are like a dream.

And like a dream the sense of rest,
That ever sweeter, fuller grows,
Broken by one white sail, that glows
A shadowy speck against the west.

ACROSS THE PARK

ACROSS the park I see the lights
Spring up with many a twinkling spark;
Like elfin eyes they gleam o' nights,
        Across the Park.

Beyond the boughs of naked trees
That lift their branches, grim and stark,
The lights of the great factories,
        Across the Park.

Wide goblin eyes, with laughter rife,
They glitter through the icy dark;
Mad eyes that mock at love and life,
        Across the Park.

HER ANSWER

"FAREWELL," she sighed, "It may not be;
Forget me — it were better so;"
The sunset heavens were all aglow,
And all on fire the sunset sea.

And rosy waves swept up the sand
To kiss the pebbles at our feet,
We saw the day and evening meet,
And yet we could not understand.

Black-robed against the tender light
She stood, a dainty silhouette;
Her bright head bowed, her lashes wet,
While gloaming deepened into night.

We heard the ocean's mournful tone
Complaining to its sandy bars;
And underneath the light of stars
She passed, and left me there alone.

TO A PHIAL OF PERFUME

TRANSLUCENT chalice, in thy crystal cell
The hoarded sweets of all the summer dwell;
    What violets gave their dewy hearts for thee,
The Angel of the Flowers alone can tell.

Gone is the scarlet rose of yesterday,
Her perfumed petals scattered to decay;
    The very soul of fragrance still abides
In thy sealed breast, and shall abide alway.

Dear messenger from lands beyond the sea,
Dreams of thy far-off country cling to thee;
    The Fatherland, that I shall never know,
Within thy limpid heart, hath come to me.

IN MEMORIAM

THE air is sweet with lilac plumes,
    And smell of violet flowers,
And roses cast their crimson blooms
    In rich and languorous showers;
And surging o'er the emerald turf,
    With lavish hand sublime,
Sweet Summer swings her blossomy surf
    Against the reefs of time.

With floating flag and martial tread
    And throb of muffled drum,
Among the peaceful soldiers, dead,
    The living soldiers come.
The heroes of a bygone day
    Still live in memory;
The boys who gave their lives away
    Shall ne'er forgotten be.

For these, no more the battle's din
    Nor trumpet's call to arms;
They rest, eternally shut in
    By God's encircling arms.
Meek dove-eyed Peace forever more
    Broods o'er each lowly bed,
And Grief herself shall e'er deplore
    Our Nation's holy dead.

Oh, soldier boys, who died for us,
    That we might live in peace,
Your sacrifice was glorious,
    Our thanks shall never cease;
Across the years, across the grave,
    We bid thee hail, again—
The Christ-like love that died to save
    Has not been given in vain.

THE DEAD YEAR

How still he lies under his robes of snow;
   Kiss his dear eyes, and cover up his face,
   And leave him in his quiet resting-place;
Dearly we loved him; we must let him go.

He brought such tender hopes and such dear dreams;
   Nay, blame him not that they are unfulfilled;
   Now that his great heart is forever stilled,
All that he planned the height of wisdom seems.

That which had made of life a Paradise,
   And all the commonplace had glorified,
   Perhaps in sovereign goodness, he denied;
And what am I to judge him less than wise?

Farewell, dear year, dearest that I have known;
   I bless thee, kneeling at thy pulseless feet;
   I shall not blush to face thee when we meet,
And stand together at the Great White Throne.

THANKSGIVING

Snow on the hills and ice upon the river,
  Mist in the valley where the sunbeams lay;
Clouds in the sky that weep as if forever
  Mourning the golden summer's vanished day.

Faintly the night wind sobs in accents weary,
  And whispering softly in the hearth's dim light,
Weird murmurs, silken rustlings vague and eerie;
  The house is full of sad-eyed ghosts to-night.

Out of the dusk gleam wraiths of vanished faces,
  And phantom hands that beckon to the past;
Dear eyes that smiled in old, familiar places,
  On other days like this, too sweet to last.

Far-away days that dearer grow and dearer,
  'Though the long years between stretch gray and
      drear;
Oh, fainting heart, give thanks! repose is nearer;
  Thy rest is nearer than it was last year.

IN "GRACE PARK"

AGAINST the faint, pale primrose of the darkening
    evening sky,
    Slender and brown the somber trees their leaf-
       less branches raise;
A flock of birds sails slowly south, with melancholy
    cry,
    And the first white star steps shyly forth, through
      the softly purple haze.

The path is beaten brown and bare, and under my
    restless tread
    The dead leaves rustle and crumble to dust with
      a sound like a wistful sigh;
And now and then one comes floating down from the
    branches overhead,
    And the wind has risen and sobs and grieves as
      it mournfully whispers by.

Good-bye, Summer! You haunted my soul wi
    dream of dear delight!
When you come again with your festal train,
    blossom and bird and bee,
And your great white moons that turn to day
    dreamy dusk of the night,
Perchance you shall smile for other eyes — I
    not be here to see.

MY CADET

HE USED to climb upon my lap
    With soft, wide eyes and eager questions,
A most engaging little chap,
    And full of curious, quaint suggestions.

And as I rocked him, half-asleep,
    His curly head against my shoulder,
I wished that I might somehow keep
    My little lad from growing older.

And now he lifts me off my feet,
    And, laughing, calls me "Little Mother;"
I wonder can it be my sweet,
    My baby boy, or just some other?

He looks so very straight and trim,
    With snowy belts and shining brasses,
So cleanly cut in brow and limb,
    A beau among the younger lasses.

He talks of "yaps" and "finning out,"
  And "plebes," and "cubs" and "kids," and
      "sneaking,"
Until, sometimes, I really doubt
  The language that my boy is speaking.

Somehow, to-night, my eyes are wet
  For baby days, so oft regretted;
And yet, I think, my big cadet,
  Is just the little lad I petted.

AN OCTOBER NIGHT

THE mist lies heavy on the landscape dear,
There are no stars to gladden this chill night;
On the dead leaves the frost rests, coldly white,
And all the clouded heaven an unshed tear.

Gone is the golden rose of yesterday,
Whose velvet petals lay against my breast;
Gone the sweet ache of summer's vague unrest,
The doubt that your dear kiss has charmed away.

Roses and stars may fade, but your divine
Caress makes summertime of all the year;
Summer forever in your kisses, dear,
Summer forever in your heart and mine.

ASHES OF ROSES

NAY, seek not under February snows
For summer's perfumed rose,
   Her petals, frail and fair,
Were long since scattered on the ambient air.
Content thee now with frost and hoary rime;
There are no roses in the winter-time.

So when Love's sun is set, and the bleak.night
Speaks still of lost delight,
   Only the soft, cold kiss
Of snowflakes whispers of departed bliss:
The crimson blooms of Love that glowed like flame,
Are scattered all and shed, a memory and a name.

A PASTORAL

WHEN crimson petals tip the rose
    And white the honeysuckle shines,
And from the garden's hushed repose
    Rises the incense of the vines;
When I would dream one sweet hour more,
My neighbor rises up at *four*.

And with his rattling old machine
    Doth vigorously chase the dawn;
In widening swaths of emerald green
    He mows the daisies on his lawn;
And nips the sweets of rising day
By turning beauty into hay.

Oh, neighbor mine, perchance your health
    Demands such sturdy exercise!
But could you take the same by stealth,
    A woman's grateful thanks would rise.
If you could manage any way
To do it later in the day.

A WOMAN'S WISH

OH, TO be young and a girl again!
Now in this girlhood of world and weather;
    Blossomy branches tap at the pane,
And my heart and the birds sing out together.
    Yellow buttercups nod in the grass,
Great furry bees are a-hum in the clover;
    Oh, for the days that come to pass
But once in a lifetime the whole world over!

    Oh, for a glimpse of the blossom time,
Sweet with the fragrance of Eden's bloom!
    Musical as the mystic rhyme,
Of brooks that ripple through starlit gloom.
    What can I give for one lost hour
Of that which seems to me half-divine?
    Oh, for the bud of life's white flower,
Whose yellowing leaf alone is mine!

IN TINTS OF GRAY

THE air is hushed and breathless;
    Before me, stretching away,
Into the dreamy shadow
    Of the closing summer day,
Lie the lake's languid waters,
    Placid and calm and gray.

Never the softest murmur
    Of a low wind whispering by,
To ruffle that tranquil bosom
    With a single rippling sigh.
Faint pearl-gray in the water,
    Faint pearl-gray in the sky.

A boat slips out of the shadow,
    Her white sails fluttering,
And one that has caught a truant beam
    Glows like a seraph's wing.
And the other reflects the dull, soft gray
    That hangs upon everything.

So we, too, glide onward,
　　Each in his devious way,
Some, perchance, to cast anchor
　　Before the close of the day;
And some of us catch the glory,
　　And some of us catch the gray.

CANONIZED

SHE knelt within the cushioned pew,
　　Her bright head bowed in prayer;
Gleams from memorial windows threw
　　A halo round her hair.
Wrapped in the whispered prayer she said,
　　Her sweet face hidden from me,
The carven seraph o'er her head,
　　Seemed not more pure than she.

Ah, happy saint! a holier light
　　Shines on thy radiant brow;
Thou hast no need, for others' plight,
　　To kneel in praying now.
The heavenly mysteries all are thine,
　　But still I wonder, dear,
If Heaven can make thee more divine,
　　Than thou wert ever here.

TWO OFFERINGS

'TWAS Easter; loud the solemn anthem rolled
Through long, dim aisles, now faintly aureoled
With dreamy tints of crimson, sapphire, emerald,
    gold.

Through dim memorial panes the softened gleam,
Flooded the gray old church with radiant stream,
And touched the pictured Christ with almost heav-
    enly beam.

The altar blazed with lights, and incense rare
Mixed with the breath of flowers, perfumed the air,
While white-robed priests softly intoned the morning
    prayer.

And sweet-voiced choristers caught up the strain,
Till all the air thrilled with the glad refrain,—
"Our Christ is risen, is risen, within our hearts
    again."

The music died to silence; sweet and low
The echo lingered, softer and more slow,
Like fluttering wings of angels, tarrying, loth to go.

Then through the scented silence, sweet and dim,
Beneath the smile of carven seraphim,
The people brought their gifts, each one as God had
       prospered him,

To the high altar; each with glad accord,
Bearing the best his substance might afford,
An offering to the temple of the Risen Lord.

And one there stepped with high and haughty mien,
Bearing an Indian pearl of dazzling sheen,
Flawless, a jewel worth the ransom of a queen.

And there was one whose steps had gone astray,
Whose feet had faltered in an evil day;
A woman who had thrown her womanhood away.

Whose face was lined with sorrow, want, and vice;
She, trembling, laid beside the pearl of price,
A spray of asphodel, that bloom of Paradise.

Long prayed the priest for her who bore the gem,
Likening her soul to the pure host of them,'
Who shine as stars in Christ's own heavenly diadem.

But with contemptuous hand swept to the ground
The flowers, whose broken petals breathed around
Delicious fragrance from each sharp and cruel wound.

So is it ever; God alone can tell,
One only gave a pearl; the asphodel
Brought Magdalene, but offered up her sorrowing
        soul as well.

THE NEW YEAR

THE light of stars drifts on the frosty air,
Above the tree-tops wreathed with plumes of snow;
In the still heaven the crescent moon hangs low;
How hushed the world is, and how wondrous fair.

He should have passed upon the wingèd storm
Who brought such wild hopes and tumultuous fears,
And colored all the vista of the years
With promises he never might perform.

O'er the white peace of the expectant earth
The midnight chimes ring out their joyous din;
Fling wide the door, welcome the New Year in;
The hour of Death hath been the hour of Birth.

What have thine untried pinions brought to me?
What crucial hour that I must face alone,
What chrism of suffering that I have not known,
What door to which I shall not find the key?

He answers not, but straightway enters in;
His eyes are homes of silent prophecy;
So the white curtain of the Time-to-Be
Sweeps down between me and my Might-have-Been.

CHÈR AMI

I KNOW a little name supremely sweet,
With dreams of love and friendship all replete,
So dear to write, such music to repeat.

All through the day 'tis singing in my breast
A little song of one I love the best;
All through the night it wakes a sweet unrest.

Dear dreams of pleasure past and joys to be,
All center, little soubriquet, in thee; —
Three little golden words, "*Mon chèr Ami.*"

AFAR OFF

SHALL we remember in some far-off day,
    When dusky tints have shadowed all the gold,
    And dull December's dreary mantle rolled
Across the glowing brightness of our May,

The hours that jealous Time too swiftly gleaned,
    And gathered in the garner of the years,
    The April smiles, the sunshine and the tears,
The rainbow from the cloud that always leaned.

The flowers of love, that we, with lavish hand,
    Flung broadcast forth, nor dreamed they e'er
        could fail;
    Flushed roses, silver lilies, faint and frail,
And passion flowers, that perfumed all the land.

Not to remember! Oh, mine eyes are wet
    That thought of such a thing could ever be—
    Nay, though Love's death itself part thee and me,
Dear heart, *dear heart*, we never can forget.

A SEASIDE FANCY

THE round white moon hangs low in the sky,
    The little winds are waking;
Upon the pebbles at our feet
    The murmuring waves are breaking;
And we two, down the silvering beach,
    Our homeward way are taking.

Her little hand upon my arm
    So lightly, lightly presses;
The fresh'ning breeze has loosened all
    Her softly flowing tresses,
And lifts them up, and kisses them,
    With tenderest caresses.

The moonbeams kiss her warm, white throat,
    Her rounded arms' soft curving;
The very pebbles kiss her feet,
    Half-shy, yet all unswerving;
All lifeless things pay homage so—
    "Love, am I less deserving?"

SONG OF THE BABY'S SHIRT

STITCH, stitch, stitch,
    In a soft, delicious dream,
A wee pearl button, a tiny loop,
    A featherstitch down a seam.

A dainty hem as wide as a straw,
    An edging of filmy lace,
And a wisp of ribbon, of baby blue,
    To fasten it all in place.

Stitch, stitch, stitch,
    Into every buttonhole,
A loving wish and a tender hope
    For the newly opening soul.

And the dainty thing as it finished lies,
    With its folds of ribbon and lace,
Calls up a dream of two soft eyes
    And a dear little dimpled face.

Stitch, stitch, stitch,
    In a tender dream beguiled,
Oh, my heart and my eyes are full to-night
    As I think of my little child.

Hide it away with loving hand,
    And a prayer in every fold,
And a clinging kiss for the dimpled thing
    That baby's shirt shall hold.

MAY TIME

SPRING hath emptied her wealth in the lap of May;
  There are handfuls of gold in the trees, in the
      clouds, in the waving grass;
There is something alive on every trembling twig and
      swinging spray,
  And something to twitter or sing in every tree
      that you pass.

All things are new and alive with a sweet new life,
  Thrilled and drenched with the gladsome sun-
      shine through and through;
The robin redbreast is building a house for his little
      brown wife,
  And the butterfly has made him a bridal bed in
      the harebell blue.

The air is full of the sweet young smell of the Spring,
  The breath of kine, and new, damp earth, and
      blossoms that blush into fruit,
And little pink buds burst forth on the boughs of the
      briar as they sway and swing,
  And the lilac is turning to purple plumes each
      slim brown spray and shoot.

The sky is blue with the blue that only comes in
    May,
    And the little gold-tinged clouds are as white as
        a far-off sail at sea;
And what of the burning stars that mark the passing
    out of the day?
    They are only an angel's dream of what to-mor-
        row's blossoms will be.

Sunshine and light and life throughout all the land,
    Cloudless heaven, and nesting bird, and blossomy
        sprig and spray;
Ah, my heart, be glad! thy springtime, too, is at
    hand,
    And thy winter-time but a far-off dream of that
        which is passed away.

SCANDAL

FOLD the sheet back softly,
  Throw the shutter wide;
Does she not look lovely?
  Smiling so, she died.

At the sunset hour,
  At the death of day,
And we thought her dreaming,
  When she passed away.

No, she did not suffer,
  Only faded so,
As the flowers wither,
  Patiently and slow.

And each morning found her
  Frailer and more weak,
Readier to leave us,
  More divinely meek.

Only one great longing
    Filled her breast alone,
Just to see your features,
    Just to hear your tone.

For she had forgiven
    All the years so long,
Darkened by suspicion,
    Jealousy and wrong.

Some things *did* look badly —
    People talked, I know,
But you'd sworn to cherish,
    And she loved you so.

And it had been nobler,
    Manlier to my mind,
Had you been more patient,
    Just a little kind.

If you had not listened
    To quite *all* they said;
Nay, I won't reproach you,
    Now she's lying dead.

Now you see as I do,
  Know her pure and true,
Do you think she knows it
  That you love her — too?

Had you written sooner —
  Ah, 'twas cruel fate,
That the word she longed for,
  Came a day *too late*.

A PANSY

STRUGGLING from darkness to day,
  Up through the heart of the mold,
Welcome, sweet daughter of May,
  Blooming in purple and gold.

What subtle instinct of life,
  Piercing thy solitude deep,
Stirred, when the storms were at strife,
  Through thy long winter of sleep.

Telling of meadow and sky,
  Fields where blonde buttercups grew,
Music of birds, and the shy,
  Passionless kiss of the dew.

Stars in the soft, summer night,
  Waters that ripple in tune,
Whispering showers, and the light,
  Fleeting caress of the moon.

Surely the hand that can trace
    Tints on a butterfly's wing,
Waked thee to radiant grace,
    Blossom of gladness and Spring.

Bloom for the broken in heart,
    Bloom for the weary and weak;
Emblem of heartsease thou art,
    Message of God to the meek.

PHOTOGRAPHS

I HAVE you in your christening robe,
    With ribbons, ruffles, lace,
And in a cotton pinafore,
    With a dirty little face.

In your first kilt. Your first wee pants,
    Carved from your daddy's own,
And on your fiery rocking-horse,
    A monarch on his throne.

And here's your faultless, first full-dress,
    For dancing, you'll believe;
And last my flawless, soldier boy
    With chevrons on his sleeve.

Each one a precious treasure, dear,
    Priceless, beyond compare;
And you are just my bonnie lad,
    Whatever clothes you wear.

A VOICE IN THE DUSK

WAILING wind and yellowing leaf,
Glimpses of sunshine pallid and brief,
Clouds that break in a sullen grief.

The warmth has faded out of the sky,
And the voice of the wind is the sound of a sigh;
Good-bye Summer, good-bye, good-bye!

Sere are the boughs of the shivering trees,
Restless trees in a fretful breeze,
Murmurous now as the moan of the seas.

Sad as the sound of a passing bell,
A tolling bell and a funeral knell;
Farewell Summer, farewell, farewell!

And love is done. 'Tis a tale that is told,
A dream that the heart may no more enfold,
A lamp burnt out, and a flame grown cold.

Over the grave of days gone by,
Let us clasp hands once, you and I,
And then forever, good-bye, good-bye!

SEPARATION

As THE long chords of some sweet symphony glide,
  Dripping like moonlit foam from delicate fingers,
So the dear thought of you sweeps into flood-tide
    Through all my empty heart, and throbs and
      lingers,
And dwells and dwells although the days divide.

Darkness and dawning, solitude and sound,
  Hold folded close the dream of your returning;
Sweet dream that thrills my loneliness profound,
    And veils with subtle sweetness my heart's yearn-
      ing;
Here shall we meet, dear heart, 'tis hallowed ground.

Come then, belovèd, for the night was long;
  Breaks the gray dawn with stormy signals flying;
Let thy dear kiss dispel the doubts that throng;
    Clasped to thy heart, my own true heart replying,
Sorrow and fear shall blossom into song.

THE MINUET

IN POWDERED hair and flowered gown,
   And patch on cheek and forehead fair,
Is there a sweeter thing in town
    In powdered hair?

Colonial beaux and belles beware!
   As Edith's partner leads her down
You're fairly rivaled, I declare.

Is this my girl with tresses brown,
   Coquettish, arch and debonaire,
Bewitching 'neath her snowy crown
    In powdered hair.

PANSIES OR LILIES

PURITAN pansies, purple eyed,
Waxen lily bells, glistening white,
  Which shall I gather to please my bride?

Lilies whose snowy cups divide
Silver gleams with the waning light;
  Puritan pansies, purple eyed.

Crystal bells where the sunbeams hide,
Pansies "for thoughts" in the solemn night;
  Which shall I gather to please my bride?

One must I choose e'er eventide —
Which shall she twine in her tresses bright?
  Puritan pansies, purple eyed?

Haste me now, for the shadows glide,
Evening smiles from her starry height;
  Which shall I gather to please my bride?

Rosy Flora could scarce decide,
How of myself can I choose aright?
  Puritan pansies, purple eyed?
  Which shall I gather to please my bride?

WHEN ROSES BUD AND LILACS BLOOM

WHEN roses bud and lilacs bloom,
　　And birds to happy birds reply,
My heart forgets its weight of gloom.

For grief can scarce find breathing room
　　Beneath the blue of such a sky,
When roses bud and lilacs bloom.

I saw it burst its chrysalis-tomb
　　The rainbow wingèd butterfly;
My heart forgets its weight of gloom.

The woods are full of faint perfume,
　　The woods will blossom, by and by,
When roses bud and lilacs bloom.

God bless the lilac's purple plume!
　　The world is glad and so am I—
My heart forgets its weight of gloom.

My soul shakes off the thought of doom
　　Nor hath she any time to sigh;
When roses bud and lilacs bloom,
My heart forgets its weight of gloom.

THAT FADED ROSE

THAT faded rose — her legacy,
Long years ago; and can it be
 The same that gleaming, pearly fair,
 Lay in her waves of raven hair,
As stars lie on a midnight sea.

She gave it flushing rosily
At my half-hesitating plea;
 Now withered, dead, it crumbles there,
 That faded rose.

There nestles close against my knee
A curly head, and full of glee
 Her children's voices thrill the air;
 But empty is the mother's chair,
And gone the hand that gave to me
 That faded rose.

A CLUSTER OF TRIOLETS

WHEN we two went a-maying
  The shadowed skies were bright;
Through leafy woodlands straying,
When we two went a-maying
And happy thought delaying
  To noonday turned the night;
When we two went a-maying
  The shadowed skies were bright.

2

Before the pallid east grew red
  She came to me with tender eyes;
Alone she stood beside my bed,
Before the pallid east grew red;
There shone a glory round her head,
  So walks she now in Paradise;
Before the pallid east grew red
  She came to me with tender eyes.

When moonlight all across my room
　　Had drifted like a silver sea,
The air was full of faint perfume;
When moonlight all across my room
Was whiter than narcissus bloom
　　My darling dead came back to me;
When moonlight all across my room
　　Had drifted like a silver sea.

4

That day in dull December
　　Still holds me with a spell;
How fondly I remember,
That day in dull December,
We watched each dying ember
　　While the gray twilight fell;
That day in dull December
　　Still holds me with a spell.

5

They mated in the early spring
　　When robins build and thrushes mate,
And nestling birds begin to sing;
They mated in the early spring,

God bless them through life's wandering,
  God grant them a most kindly fate;
They mated in the early spring
  When robins build and thrushes mate.

6

Before the rosy west grew gray
  And lengthening shadows dimmed the sky,
We waited for the death of day;
Before the rosy west grew gray
We put a tender hope away,
  And stood apart and saw it die;
Before the rosy west grew gray,
  And lengthening shadows dimmed the sky.

I

When baby first came
  He was only *so* long,
Too small even to name;
When baby first came,
But for love he'd a claim
  That grew strong and more strong,
When baby first came
  He was only *so* long.

II

The baby's pink fist
    That closed round my finger,
A thing to be kissed
The baby's pink fist,
And the fat, dimpled wrist,
    So to kiss it I linger,
The baby's pink fist,
    That closed round my finger.

III

The baby's blue eyes
    'Neath their long, silken fringes,
So round and so wise
The baby's blue eyes,
They've the hue of the skies,
    With the twilight's soft tinges;
The baby's blue eyes
    'Neath their long, silken fringes.

IV

A curl of the baby's hair
    In a little, old-fashioned locket,
Shining, yellow and fair,
A curl of the baby's hair

Is a jewel beyond compare
    As I fondle it down in my pocket,
A curl of the baby's hair
    In a little, old-fashioned locket.

HER DREAMING EYES

HER dreaming eyes, with gaze serene,
Through all the years that intervene,
    Still smile from out the carven frame,
    As in the days when first she came
To be my love, my life, my queen.

The wingèd seasons drift between,
The winter's snow, the summer's green;
    They're but a memory and a name,
        Her dreaming eyes.

Her winsome face, her girlish mien,
Still from the glowing canvas lean;
    And in my heart she dwells the same,
    Hallowed by Love's immortal flame,
Though years are fled since I have seen
        Her dreaming eyes.

IN SUMMER TIME

In SUMMER time when skies were blue,
The world seemed made for just us two,
  A paradise, before unknown,
  Through which we wandered all alone,
As quite shut out from mortal view.

You lived for me and I for you,
All else seemed vague, unreal, untrue,
    You were my queen, my heart your throne,
      In summer time.

And now, that summer days have flown,
The tender hope hath sweeter grown,
    For as the swift days swifter flew,
    We found we could not say adieu,
And I shall claim you all my own,
      In summer time.

LOVE AND I

LOVE went hand in hand with me,
  Through the sunlit hours;
Summer smiled on land and sea,
  Wreathed the world with flowers.

  Blossom-laden bowers
Beckoned us from lawn and lea;
Love went hand in hand with me
  Through the sunlit hours.

Still my royal guest is he,
  Though the winter lowers;
Still on golden pinions flee
  Sunny days and showers;
Love went hand in hand with me
  Through the sunlit hours.

THISTLEDOWN

THISTLEDOWN, airy and slight,
    Far from the dust of town,
Clad in thy garments white,
    Thistledown.

Changing thy purple gown,
    Beautiful proselyte,
For a novice's snowy crown.

Fading and lost in a night,
    All but thy calyx brown,
Emblem of all that is bright,
    Thistledown.

LOVE PASSES BY

LOVE passes by in airy flight,
    E'er yet we deemed him nigh;
In all the longing heart's despite,
      Love passes by.

We hear, perchance, a tender sigh,
    A shadow veils the sight;
The white winged doves drift past on high.

So life doth miss life's best delight,
    When swift as song-birds fly,
Nor bending from his heavenly height,
      Love passes by.

"THE PLAY'S THE THING"

"THE Play's the thing," wherein to snare
    More than the conscience of a king;
Thoughts deep as Death or light as air—
    "The Play's the thing."

All moods, all types, their tribute bring;
    Gathered within the footlight's glare,
Full-rounded as a golden ring.

Wild jealousy and mad despair,
    And Love that mounts on azure wing,
All things that are or ever were,
    "The Play's the thing."

THINE EYES

THINE eyes have drawn my heart, my soul,
  As lingering moonbeams draw the sea;
  I know not yet what love may be;
I own the might of love's control.

I crown thee with the aureole
  Of love's unuttered mystery;
Thine eyes have drawn my heart, my soul,
  As lingering moonbeams draw the sea.

What magic through my being stole
  When thy deep glance enveloped me;
A boundless ocean seemed to roll,
  My all was swallowed up in thee;
Thine eyes have drawn my heart, my soul,
  As lingering moonbeams draw the sea.

HESITATION

WHAT I would say remains unsaid,
  Still unexpressed from day to day;
A tangled skein, a broken thread,
  What I would say.

Love chafes against this vain delay;
  The wingèd hours, forever fled,
Return not, howsoe'er we pray.

I am thine own; I bow my head
  To thy mute question, and obey;
Have thy deep eyes interpreted
  What I would say?

TO THE BELOVÈD

THE thought of you fills all the difficult day;
    I wonder where you are and whom you meet,
    And all my meditations, memory-sweet,
Pause on you, dear; so near, yet far away.
The hours drag by, employ them as I may;
    The lagging hours that creep with leaden feet,
    And all the day, empty and incomplete,
Withers to twilight, desolate and gray.

So day and twilight take their heavy flight;
    The past returns with all its hopes and fears,
      And every dear remembrance wakes anew;
I live again in every lost delight,
    Till the night falls and sleep seals up my tears;
      Most blessèd sleep, with its long dreams of
      you.

MARCH

A WINDY day! perhaps a chance
    Some faultless hosiery to display,
And *lingerie*, direct from France,
    A windy day.

Shall I discreetly look away,
    Or steal one more admiring glance,
At such a charming disarray?

Cascades of lace retreat, advance,
    What silken pleats, what ruffles gay,
All whirled in an impromptu dance.
    A windy day.

A BABY'S EYES

A BABY'S eyes, like violets blue,
   Or twin lakes under summer skies,
How soft they peep and smile at you,
     A baby's eyes.

The long curled lashes fall and rise,
   O'er those sweet orbs of heaven's own hue,
In tantalizing compromise.

Two harebells, wet with early dew,
   Two stars through twilight's dusky guise,
Shine not so fair to mortal view,
     As baby's eyes.

HER EASTER HAT

HER Easter hat is wide of rim,
A wreath of poppies clasps its brim,
　　With knots of wheat and creamy lace;
　　And underneath her charming face
Dimples in shadow soft and dim.

A hornèd beetle, green and grim,
Disports his shining wing and limb,
　　Upon the wreath whose buds embrace
　　　Her Easter hat.

Methinks, it is a curious whim,
What beauty can she see in him?
　　And yet to win her gentle grace,
　　In her dear heart to own a place,
I'd be a bug, and help to trim—
　　　Her Easter hat.

MY SWEETHEART

My sweetheart is but six years old,
  Yet oh, an arch-coquette is she:
Aglint her brown locks are with gold,
  And green her eyes are, as the sea.

Her throne she finds upon my knee,
  Where all her luring wiles unfold;
  My sweetheart is but six years old,
Yet oh, an arch-coquette is she.

To snatch a kiss I'd fain be bold,
  From lips that pout provokingly;
Her trusty knight am I enrolled,
  She is indeed my fair lady;
My sweetheart is but six years old,
  Yet oh, an arch-coquette is she.

IN THE SUBURBS

OH, FOR a breath of summer!
   Well, it's beginning again;
Spring, you're a very late comer,—
   Oh, for a pause in the rain!

Well, its beginning again,
   Drizzle and drizzle and drizzle;
Oh, for a pause in the rain,
   Spring, you're a cheat and a fizzle!

Drizzle and drizzle and drizzle,
   Oh, for a sight of the sun!
Spring, you're a cheat and a fizzle,
   You'll be over before you've begun.

Oh, for a sight of the sun!
   After this dropping and dripping;
You'll be over before you've begun,
   Spring, with your slopping and slipping.

After this dropping and dripping
   The wet gets into one's brain;
Spring, with your slopping and slipping,
   We've had quite enough of the rain.

The wet gets into one's brain,
   And the damp gets into one's temper;
We've had quite enough of the rain!
   Tyrannus, and also *sic semper*.

The damp gets into one's temper
   (Drip go the drops on the pane),
Tyrannus, and also *sic semper*,
   Oh, for the sunshine again!

Drip go the drops on the pane,
   Spring, you're a very late comer!
Oh, for the sunshine again,
   Oh, for a breath of the Summer!

SISTER LOUISE

SHE kneels apart in her sad-colored gown,
  Clasping her carven beads,
With her meek head bowed and her eyes cast
    down,
Under their fringes, darkest brown,
  On the printed prayer she reads.

No faintest shadow of sorrow or sin,
  On that lovely, passionless face;
Pale as the linen under her chin,
Only the heaven she strives to win,
  Claims in her heart a place.

Sanctified, sealed, and set apart!
  I wonder if still in her breast
Beats one faint pulse of a woman's heart
That sometimes makes her tremble and start,
  With a nameless, vague unrest.

If, sometimes, deep in the midnight hush
  Those beautiful eyes are wet,
And that pale cheek flames with a sudden flush,
At the thoughts her strong will cannot crush—
  At the days she can never forget.

II

Alone with *me* in that star-lit place
  As Adam and Eve were alone,
With my lips close-pressed to her fair, flushed
    face,
And she yielded herself to my close embrace,
  Body and soul my own!

My regiment sailed at dawn that day,
  But the moon dropped out of the sky,
And the faint stars flickered and faded away,
And the east was streaked with a pallid gray,
  Before we could say "good-bye."

I left her then for the field of strife,
  Left her for half-a-year,
And I swore as I hoped for a future life,
That when I came back I'd make her my wife,
  I came, and I found her—here.

Then I knew why her letters ceased
    And why mine were returned unread;
She used to confess to a sleek, young priest,
Perhaps her heart failed as the days increased,
    And she harkened to what he said.

God forgive him! All thought of blame
    Centers forever there;
For he prated to her of a tarnished name
Till the maddening sense of her guilt and shame,
    Was more than her strength could bear.

III

And now as I gaze on her kneeling there
    Telling her wooden beads,
With her downcast eyes and suppliant air
And the somber veil on her beautiful hair
    My whole heart trembles and bleeds.

If she had waited a little! Ah, well,
    It's too late for her now to complain;
She's fettered for life — but who can tell?
I'd pit my soul against Heaven or Hell
    To win her over again.

To snatch her out of that sanctified place,
    She, the Bride of the Skies,
And soothe away every sorrowful trace,
And kiss the color back to her face,
    And the light to her beautiful eyes.

For the time will come when early and late,
    The thought of what might have been,
Will haunt and goad till she'll learn to hate
The living death she chose for her fate,
    When she thought she was tired of sin.

Some night when the moonlight floods the trees
    With its arrows of silver rain,
And the slender branches bend in the breeze,
The nun shall ask for Sister Louise—
    And, seeking, shall seek in vain.

    L. of C.

SONG

Oh, the sweet summer-time,
  All the world is green;
Red rose and white rose,
  Set in emerald sheen;
Lilac plume and fragrant bloom,
  Freighting branch and bough.
Welcome, Sweetheart,
  Sweetheart, welcome now.

Oh, the somber autumn-time,
  All the world is brown;
Dry leaf and dead leaf,
  Drifting sadly down.
Gray cloud and misty shroud,
  Veiling earth and sky;
Good-bye, Sweetheart,
  Sweetheart, good-bye!

APRÉS

HOW SHALL I face you under alien eyes,
  After that kiss?
How shall I frame you commonplace replies
  With my heart full of this—
  Hour of ecstatic bliss?

How shall I greet you? Will the garish light
  Dim these poor charms,
Or will you find me fair, as when last night,
  Thrilling with sweet alarms
  I trembled in your arms?

Morning and noon and night, dear heart, the same
  In love's own book.
How shall I tremble but to hear your name,
  Meeting your steadfast look,
  Knowing the kiss you took.

AFTERMATH

Heart of a rose with all its crimson sweetness,
　　Mystery of starlight asleep upon the sea;
Promise of the harvest in its rich completeness,
　　Fullest fruition in the days to be; —
　　That's what the summer-time means to me.

Heart of my heart, and end of all desiring,
　　Night-dream and day-dream still return to thee;
Eyes of you, and hands of you, and lips of you, be-
　　　　lovèd,
　　Love's dear fulfillment in the days to be; —
　　That's what the summer-time means to me.

IN MEMORIAM

SPRING hath come back, with all her festal train,
  With all her tender dreams and memories,
And the old sorrow buds and blooms again,
  And bears its blossoms with the blossoming
        trees,—
Its bitter fruit of unforgotten pain.

A nation's sorrow for a nation's loss,
  The flower of all her chivalry cut down;
The martyr throng that bore the heavy cross
  The radiant host that wears the unfading crown

How still they sleep within their tents of green
  Whose breasts once thrilled to hear the bugle's
        note,
Whose pulses leaped to meet the challenge keen
  Flung from the brazen cannon's awful throat.

We lay our wreaths upon their graves to-day,
  With hearts that ache; but not for these alone
Who rest, their triumph won, their names alway,
  On memory carved, as on the unyielding stone.

Rather for those who war for eternal peace,
  The unnumbered hosts that still must face the
        strife;
The heroes of unblazoned victories,
  The palmless conquerors on the field of Life.

A SILENT SINGER

ALL her life long she hoped for happier days,
   When one mistake made all her world go wrong;
She drooped, a flower denied its sun-god's rays,
   All her life long.

Men wondered at the sadness of her song,
   The tremor in the nightingale's soft lays,
The minor chord in notes so sweet and strong.

Indifferent alike to blame or praise,
   Careless she moved amid the careless throng;
Only her God knows of her lonely ways,
   All her life long.

IN HADES

They speak of Hell as of a place of flame,
Wherein men expiate their sin and shame;
   Where all the ill that they have done on earth
Is purified by suffering without name.

To feel the lack of all we count most dear,
The agony of alternate hope and fear,
   To wait and wait, and always still to wait
For that which never comes, and Hell is here.

FINIS

ASHES to ashes, dust to dust,
   Ashes of love and dust of desire,
Folded away with the moth and rust,
   All that is left of fuel of fire.

Dust of dreams that faded in night,
   Ashes of hearts that were all aflame;
Hide them away with the mold and blight,
   Only a memory and a name.

Ashes to ashes, dust to dust,
   Shrouded in darkness let them be;
Ashes of hope and faith and trust,
   All that your friendship left to me.